I0148809

Minnehaha Falls

Dr. Greg Nielsen

Conscious Books
316 California Ave., Ste 210
Reno, Nevada 89509
U.S.A.

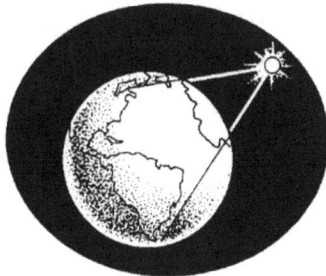

ISBN 978-0-9619917-6-0

Email: spiritualfrequenciesonline@gmail.com

Instagram: drgfrequencies

X (formerly Twitter): @FrequenciesDrG

YouTube: Greg Nielsen@DrG1

Additional digital books, video, and audio including podcasts go to:
Patreon.com/spiritualfrequencies

Venmo: contribute directly to Conscious Books and Spiritual Frequencies Online Academy: @Greg-Nielsen-9

Conscious Books
316 California Ave. Ste 210
Reno, Nevada 89509
U.S.A.

Other Poetry and Books by Dr. Greg Nielsen

Light Waves in the book Tuning to the Spiritual Frequencies

RiverSpeak

Available on Amazon.com

Star Consciousness: Direct, Manage & Transform Your Energy

Gateway to Stardust: How to Resonate with Natural Order Frequencies
&
Mythological Themes in Art, Literature and Tattoos

Minnehaha Falls

Feeling the frozen spray
The last fire
No tourists
Along the creek,
Maybe after the solstice.

Youthful memories plunge,
Neurons resonating
Rippling cells
Become brainwave.

I like visiting The Falls
When no one is there
Nature's intimacy
The water is in between
Frozen and liquid.

Memories skip and hop,
In one month
Or two months
The Falls will be a wall
Of water ice jewels.

The silent north chill
Skin, nerves, and thoughts
Slower thoughts can be easier
To turn, rotate, revolve
Holographic perspectives.

In the dead of winter
There's abundant life
Behind the Shady Way Roadhouse
An icy swamp, brown but alive
It's quiet in the house.

Everyone is gone
At 20 below I dress warm
I venture into the frozen swamp
As a hunter stalking game
No frogs or crickets.

Small birds chirp
Occasionally I see a white rabbit
I feel the Wayzata Indians
Who hunted in this swamp
Well over 100 years ago.

The dead of winter is not so dead
What is dead
But alive in disguise
Wearing frozen cattail makeup
With icicle tear jewelry.

I nestle down
Behind an Indian mound.
I wait patiently for a bird
A bird impatiently lands
On a frozen brown cattail.

The snow beneath my bones
Is the mouth of Minnehaha Creek.

Only the ghosts of the Dakota
Know the spring ice melting
Flowing into Lake Minnetonka.

When I was 10 Rusty
Was hit by a dump truck
At highway 12 and 101
He died instantly
I cried agony.

Buried in our Shady Way
Back yard, his decay
Drained into the swamp
Microscopic cocker spaniel
Feeding Minnehaha waters.

I took aim, chickadee
No bow, no arrow, no soul
The white hunter killer
That senselessly slaughtered
The buffalo, sadly even the white buffalo.

I read 100 books
That winter of below zero
My mind was summer all winter
With words, stories, non-fiction
For Whom the Bell Tolls, Great Gatsby.

You can watch the journey
On YouTube, Three teen dudes
Taco Bell, burritos, canoe from
Lake Minnetonka to Minnehaha Falls.

22 miles downstream
https://www.youtube.com/watch?v=l93hUHQKlU0
It feels like a timeless adventure
Swamp, creek, lake, falls
Feeling the frozen splash.

When it snowed on Shady Way
Above the dry, crackling swamp.
Glad we had TV and books
And an active imagination
With National Geographic.

Loved the maps
Sailed the Caribbean
Photo journaled from island to island.
Explored the Carlsbad Caverns
Mysterious underworld.

In spring, kissed Minnehaha Creek
Waters thawing
The Creek surged into Minnetonka
Cast the line
Sunfish splashed ashore.
Melting Itasca snow
Ice in March
Water in May
Minnehaha, Mississippi,
Minnetonka, Minneapolis.

Summer, beaches, and water skiing
Excelsior Amusement Park

Lafayette Country Club
Picnic at Minnehaha Falls
Fishing for Pike and Walleye.

Minnesota, 10,000 Lakes
30,000 streams and creeks
50,000 swamps
Mosquitos and blackbirds
Sun, humidity, thick sweat.

Barbeque, corn on the cob
Steak, burgers, and hot dogs
Mustard, ketchup, relish
Labor Day barbeque sauce,
Fall in the air.

Late autumn, first snow
The swamp whispers,
"Visit Minnehaha"
Freezing boil
Between water and ice.

The first freeze
Cold at Minnehaha
No one there
A peaceful visit
Despite the icy wind.
I still sleep on Minnehaha ice
Covered in snowy powder
Destiny visions
Past-Present-Future-Now
Feeling the voltage in the vortex.

Poems from 9th grade – 5-25-65

Here and Now

Ah, those lingering years of learning past
A dozen moments it seems, imbedded now
Upon a solid step and I stand fast
Naïve and apathetic; "World I bow."

Above – or possibly below, another stop
Upon another step which singled out
Made firm by constant wear of annual crop
A last moment to decide, do not doubt.

And from what knowledge I have gained thus far
Eve' though minute in manner and detail
I must decide upon my distant star
For all wandering steps will surely fail.

So, say I climb not each step without thought
But choose your way not by what others sought.

Comments

The signs unknown, unrealized yet
While journeys ended and more ahead
And milestones reached and others passed by
Some seen, some sensed not to forget
While others lost forever

A sudden changing wind has whispered to me and
spoke
Lost in a place out beyond the visible sky
To chance upon again? Never – never.

Must tranquility and security measure the success
Of life ended and life to come.
Will only material possessions represent achievements?
What purpose do the intangible things possess?
Like imagination, love, and happiness

Napkin Poem

My heart is your heart
Beating in time
In Rhyme
Fine hearts
Together, Weather
Storms brewing
Wind Drinking
My/Your Heart.

Windy
Rainy-Sunny
Silent
Independent
Yet together
Live-once
Love-more
Silence.

Summer of Love, 1967

Postcard found in a bathroom
Torn from the aged walls
A cornerstone treasure mailed
Like a seed transported.

Jungle Vino

Meet me at the Vino on First
Next to the Truckee River.
Sip the red & white wines
From grapes around the world.

Welcome to the tasting
Enjoy the flight
With friends and lovers and strangers.

The appetizers delight
Especially the cheddar, Swiss and Brie.
Try the gourmet pizza.
There's beer on tap.

Listen to rap and poetry.
Set your eyes on paintings,
Drawings and photography.

Meet me at the Vino.
Stop on by.

Drink the beer.
Sip the wine.
You'll love
The atmosphere.

Red Rock

A bar on Sierra Street
In Reno's heart
Where young & old meet
To enjoy wine, beer & art.

See you at Red Rock,
I'll buy you a drink.
It's just down the block,
Nearer than you think.

The espresso is the finest
In Reno town.
It's truly the best
You'll find anywhere around.

From happy hour to close
You'll never be blue.
It takes away your woes
May the Rock be with you.

The Hub

Grind the bean
Pull a shot,
The Hub's the scene
Where the coffee's hot.
Cappuccino or espresso,
Macchiato or latte,
An Americano
Or the coffee of the day.
The organic coffee grows
In Ethiopia or Brazil
Or where the water flows
Down a Central American hill.
Good conversation and coffee,
The Hub where friends meet
To share a specialty
On Cheney Street.

Silver Peak

A restaurant called Silver Peak
Where I eat each week.
Got a deck with a view
Of Mt. Rose's pink hue.

Got the best food in town,
Every day, all year round.
Got the burgers and fries.
Salads, entrees, and pizza pies.

They brew their own beers
With magic, smoke, and mirrors.
Let the good times roll
On the Wonder Street knoll.

You're invited to the party
Where the brew is light and hearty.
Let The Peak be your host
For a cheer, salud, skoll or a toast.

Hell No

Selective Service number 21-50-48-193
Viet-Nam, Draft.
Local Board No. 50
Hennepin County, September 1, 1966.

Hell no, I won't go,
Hell no, I won't go,
Hell no, I won't go.

April 1967, Market Street
San Francisco
Bell bottoms, hippies
Haight Ashbury
Daffodils, roses
Burning sticks of incense
Protest Echoes

Hell no, we won't go
Hell no, we won't' go
Hell no, we won't go.

Several students appeared
On campus Friday
Handing out underground leaflets.
They advocated the repeal
Of existing marijuana and drug laws.

Hell no, we won't go,
Hell no, we won't go,
Hell no, we won't go.

Students protested
The appearance of a recruiter
For Dow Chemical Company,
Manufacturer of Napalm
For the Vietnam War.
Protestors took over
The University President's office.

Hell no, we won't go,
Hell no, we won't go,
Hell no, we won't go.

Written for my brother the night before the funeral

Michael

The sun slept, awoke, and the earth shivered.
The clouds scraped against sandpaper sky,
Exploding raindrops across the yellowing lawn.
Birds soared, gliding toward the sheltered lake.

Peace froze the lake to bond the shores,
Blanketing frigid forms beneath.
Sealed anew in the vault of contentment,
Michael whispers life's beauty in muffled echoes.

Vivid memories of him are locked,
Fondling the pages of my diary
And etching scribbled symbols of his love and joy
On the parchment of ancient scrolls.

More fragrant the flowers blossoming in spring
And kiss the sky good morning in friendship
To the warm winds that caressed laughing waves,
And soon will they splash again upon the beaches.

Hell No, He Won't Go

Hell no, he didn't go,
Hell no, he didn't go,
Hell no, he didn't go.

Where are we living?
Let we ask a question about
The space tradition.
Where are we living?
Behind the sun?

Is he dead?
Or does he know now?
Did he see him buried or born?
Coffined in the grave,
Is he in there really, decaying?

Doctor pronounced him dead,
Funeral director produced him buried.
Rhetoric and a movie.
Oh, what a light show.
Like the one we see
At the center of consciousness.

To see him first
Dead on the bed
Hole in his head.
He loved too much,
Too much I said,
"You idiot," feeling his pulse
None. The bleeding of my heart
None. The bleeding of our heart
None. The beating, beating, beating.
Some.

In the spring of 1969
He developed leukemia.
He was extensively studied
At the hematology department
Of the University of Minnesota
Medical School.

The treatment was primarily
Transfusion, cortisone, and androgens.
Over the next six months
He made gradual recovery.
By July 1970, he recovered
His bone marrow function
Signed Dr. Cabot Wohlrabe.

Hell no, I didn't go,
Hell no, I didn't go,
Hell no, I didn't go

Dada and the Sun

Nova

Nova, bright darkness
The death of it you know
Star explosion and the scatter
Through the universe.

Matter and light tumbling
Through space, in space, outer

Space. One thousand light years
From the rock and rumble.

Too brilliant to see
Like sun dancing with snow
In the spotlight – Love
At first sight – Nova.

Spacewalk

The slumber, rolled over soon,
Playing dead in a dream at dawn.
I ran beside a highway
Along a rocky shore – gone
To the valleys of the moon.

Time spins wedlocked
In capsules of speed.
The weightless whisper,
"Wedlocked with Freedom" – Free – Freed.
I sojourned with death un-clocked.

The night, the dark,
The agony of the sea.
A breeze arises from the shore
To frolic passed the vision of me.
I walk, tumble, stark

Step, the sands press
Like open hands, bare feet.

It tickles and the laughing
Beach subdued – the best
The lapping, lapping – recess.

No one knows of no one
Here, alone under the light.
To search, to seek, to see
The morning, dart back – bright,
The vision of me, the sun.

Passing Over California

When walking beneath a redwood,
California is not so far away.
The redskins are sending out smoke signals,
We see them passing overhead.

Tall redwood of the city
Sending out packages of smoke.
The sun ties a bow around you.
You are a present stripped bare,
Your giant branches are buildings
Erected and demolished.

If we all together wrapped
Our hands around you, we would
Feel your breadth, but none
Are tall enough to untie the bow
Except the sun when
Passing over California.

Pieces of Darkness

Pieces of darkness dashing
Through a morning fog
And all the streetlights were on
Casting shadows into the eyes of
Paper doll phantoms on parade.

One, she was the innocent,
God's only begotten daughter sent
Instead of the son, to push
Big Ben up one time zone where
You and I began
In the lilac bush in your
Father's garden.

Breathing pieces of darkness
At 20,000 leagues beneath the pavement
He lashed you with paper shadows
And shined streetlights in your
Eyes, forcing the lilac into your nostrils.

I ate the lilac and was sick
Like when I ate pizza on the dock.
I heaved two times on a wave
Crossing the street on a red light.

Behind the Sun

Let we ask a question about
The space tradition.
Where are we living,
Behind the Sun?

Once

Once he was happy, like Christ
He was on the porch in fall
Through the door and out
He said, "Hey Baby" blowing
A kiss to the world and all
The leaves rustled – I
Kissed him back.

Long Haired Monsters

Women are long haired monsters
Come to play.
We are ready and pretending.
Hocus-Pocus-Magic-Light-Switch off.

Long haired monsters jumping like frogs
In and out of light switches they come
Like an electric shock, we come
Ready and pretending, we are
Long haired monsters come to play.

Landing on the moon we step
Out on the earth.
Dada and the Sun
My dog has human eyes –
Because she stares at me.
Clytemnestra, we call her –
Come here.

She was our Zen teacher,
Flipping flapjacks for breakfast
To explain the existence of the sun.
Here dada is the sun.

And more- She was our master
When I, a Greek slave, roamed
The countryside in evening listening
To the silence, distant purrs and
Shrills of a city whispered in tongues.
We understood nothing
Of the silence except
We heard.

Silo

Counting the silos, moving
In the distance – they are near
Barns in clumps of trees.
Driving, the morning was a silo painted yellow
On our side of the road
We counted the morning a silo.

Love Creation

When a man and a woman
Hold and hug
Each other
In love,
Another universe
Is created.
Souls come into
Being.
You are their
Creators.
When a man and a woman
Love,
They love
Their creations
And the souls
They created
Love them.
The rush
Of energy,
A man
And a woman
Feel.
When they hold and hug
Each other
In love,
Is the same
Feeling
God-Goddess felt

When they created
This universe.

Tracy

I love you very much;
You have a lovely touch.
You are a goddess to me
Strong, sensitive, and free.
I love talking with you;
Everyday it's new.
You have the energy of light
Radiating golden bright.
I hold you in my heart
Even when we are apart.
I wish you True romance
Sharing life's eternal dance.

Love Song to Cyndee

My heart sings a song
A serenade
To the one I love,
Always a soul friend,
Always a soul mate.
It's a warm spring day
When I'm with you.
My heart is a golden lotus
Fragrant with lasting love.

Blossomed petals hold you
With the gently strength
Of true love.
Listening to the melody
Our hearts sing
In resonant harmony
We walk hand in hand
Into a timeless temple
Where brightly color flowers
Grow spontaneously
Out of thin air
Bearing witness
To the integrity
Of our love.

Love Sonnet 1

Your radiant face lights my heart
With happiness and joy
And when you smile my lips part
Beaming back words not coy.

Love is light blue in your eyes
Where I can see the sky ever fair
And your soul's passage, joys, and cries
Through the ages of love and despair.

Such fine hair sweet beauty
Hath no man caressed
To touch it is to forget duty
And become lost in love's nest.

Love reflected in refined features
Tells more than all Wisdom's teachers.

Love Sonnet 2

What kind of heart hath love?
Strong, nourishing, healing, soft.
All of these my angel dove
Lifts your heart's wings aloft.

Your gentle strength reassures
When manly confidence wanes.
Your nourishing warmth endures
Despite heart's winter and icy pains.

There's healing in your heart
Brings back from death's swallow
And then a soft part
A pillow to my thoughts hollow.

Be thankful for a love defined
Imagination is no heart but mind.

Love Sonnet 3

Beauty is the form love takes
When the eye of the beholder sees
Then the heart-feel awakes
A slumbering love breeze.

The wind of love is gentle
Never blowing, never gusting
A soft zephyr-feeling, not mental,
Not desire, passion, or lusting.

Your form is beauty love-honey.
My heart is carried by a wind,
A current gentle and sunny
Beyond mortal emotion and mind.

Beauty is not an image but form
Sculpted by Love winds warm.

Love Sonnet 4

Your very presence is lightness
Lifts me from mortal weight
Your aura radiates a brightness
Takes away every negative state.

I have seen your angel wings,
Golden fans spread in flight
Swift motion so that air sings
Of your radiance, love, and light.

I love you angel, very much
That I want to fly with you
And reach out, gently touch
Loving each other anew.

Love is a lifting lightness
Bringing an aura brightness.

RiverSpeak 42 - River in My Ears

River flows rapidly through my ears
Washing my soul with sound.
Clinging and clutching,
Thoughts and feelings are swept
Into the cosmic sea.
Before I was more like rock.
Now I'm more like water.
River flows rapidly through my ears;
It's soothing sound,
Both soft and energizing,
Quiets me inside.
The silence is more powerful
Than thunder and lightning
Rocking the summer evening sky.
I'm peaceful in the
Center of the storm.
Listening to the river
Flowing rapidly through my ears
Has opened my eyes.

RiverSpeak 85 - Counting on River

I can count on River
Flowing to the sea

For a timeless eternity,
Spinning, whirling
Spiraling energy.
The force of water
Cutting and carving
In earth, through earth
Into the bowels of earth.
Water is soft
Yet it cuts
Through rock hard granite.
The force of water
Puts out the force of fire.
River flows to the sea;
You can count on that.
Wet, wild mighty river
Crashes into giant waves
Water against water,
An explosion of water.
The force of water squared.
I can count on River.

Light Wave 93

Caught in action's craze,
Blind in a life maze;
Running, rushing, doing,
No time for rest-reviewing.

Stop the mind greed dance,
Give yourself a chance;

Make time for light-tune
Feel the spiritual boon.

Alternate action-rest,
That seems to be the best;
Keeps you stable and strong,
Your cells singing a song.

Light Wave 78

The cosmic process is all in all,
You cannot walk before you crawl;
I this and I that,
A diet of 'I' s makes us fat.

Consciously cooperate,
Fulfill your functional fate;
Work according to the plan,
Each child, woman, and man.

Face the facts squarely,
They will judge you fairly;
The truth shall set you free,
Try it once or twice, you'll see.

Light Wave 65

Across the sea of light,
Of transparent golden-white;

On a ship with solar sails
Passed giant cosmic whales.

Hands of unrelenting will
Holds the golden wheel still;
Forever manning the helm,
Toward the light being realm.

Reaching the edge of divine night
Cosmic presence wields its might
Dissolves individual form,
Cosmic consciousness born.

Light Wave 75

Love knows only giving,
Wisdom practices living;
Will applies the power,
Balance the three each hour.

False love expects returns,
False wisdom book learns,
False will is selfish desire,
Unbalanced forces expire.

Give conscious love,
Wisdom comes from above,
Will is measured action,
Make whole the three-fold fraction.

Buffalo Bill (4th grade, 1958)

Buffalo Bill was kind and good,
He liked to help all people.
He liked to hunt the buffalo.
He knew and loved the trails.
He liked to be an army scout,
To help his country out.
When he was old, he told the young
The adventures he had when he was young.

Buffalo and River

I put my ear
To the earth
There are pounding sounds
On the horizon
Buffalo feet running
In a great herd
Across the earth
They are thirsty together.
They are looking for river
River twists and turns
The buffalo are thirsty
For her water.
The buffalo pound the earth
Sending a message to river
"Where are you?
We are thirsty."
The river twists and turns toward the buffalo,

"You are welcome
To drink my water."

White Buffalo

There is a
White Buffalo
Grandfather saw it
Once in a dream
He told me,
"It stood on the
Hill alone staring
At me with deep
Lake blue eyes
Our minds joined.
His thoughts told
Me a secret
He said 'There's a
Great white light
Surrounding your body.
All the buffalo
See it glowing.
As long as you are one
With the spirit
The great white light
Grows
Then I woke up.
The White Buffalo
Was gone.
There were always
Enough buffalo

After that
As long as I was one
With the spirit."
Grandfather was
Chief
For a very long time.

Wind, Sky, Eagle, Buffalo

The Wind blows
The Sky blue
Earth warms
With sunshine.
The Eagle is a friend
The Buffalo runs.
The Wind and the Sky
The Earth and the Sun
Together they Sun rise
Lighting the medicine path.
The Eagle gives you a feather
The Buffalo gives you a blanket.
The Wind and sky are invisible.
They are indivisible.
The Spirit is one
Everywhere.

Moon

Moon has many faces:
She can be
Happy and bright
Sad and dark,
Or some of both.
Moon's light
Is always changing
She does not shine
Steady like her father
Sun.
Moon likes to dance.
When she's full
She dances on water
On leaves and in the
Eyes of night animals.
Moon doesn't like to dance
When she's dark and empty
She hides her face.
Father sun cannot
Cheer her up.
The water leaves
And night animals
Have no dancing partner.
When she uncovers her
Face
She is crescent moon.
Her mood is moderate
Then distant stars
Are attracted by
Her smile.

Pine Tree

Ever-green
Many seasons growing
Beside lake.
In winter
The water freezes
Pine tree
Stays warm
Wrapped in a green blanket.
The forest animals
Seek shelter
In a snowstorm
Under Pine Tree
After the big snow
They come out and play
Pine Tree wears a new
White dress
The forest animals
Admire her beauty.
In the summer Pine Tree
Does not wear
A white dress.

Fire

The Fire warms
Cold hands
And feet.

It cooks the deer
And the buffalo.
The dancing flames
Flicker and spark.
The stars are Fires
Burning in the night.
A great chief
Lights them
And feeds them wood
Until the sun rises.
The Fire keeps us
From dying.
We would die
Without Fire.
Fire is our friend
As long as we feed Fire.
When we stop feeding Fire
Fires goes out.
Our hands and feet freeze.

Haikus

Elbowologist
Tickles my funny bone
I wear short sleeve shirts.

I just haven't met
The perfect woman for me
Thank God I am still free.

Will I be happy
When I fall in love?
I am happy now!

Marriage maniacs
Think they are superior.
To singles like me.

Listen to the waves
Walking barefoot in the sand
Feel ocean inside.

It's time to get up
Now it's time to go to sleep
Sleepwalking all day.

I am daydreaming
About the perfect woman
I have a girlfriend.

Went to lunch alone
And she said, "just one today?"
Alone, not lonely.

Upside down backwards
The north side of the south pole
The bottom of top.

Pipe organ sound thrill
Fills the church, a bodily chill
River flows outside.

A stroke of good luck
A near death experience
Have health insurance.

Grow the bean, roast, grind
Pull the shot Ethiopia
Sipping Gaia.

My heart feels your soul
Connection to your sweet self
My heart to your heart.

Woman in Light

We love forever. Our souls are friends.
We help each other return to the light.
When I look at you, I see many
Lives across time sing in my heart.
We have and will share everything.
What is mine is yours.
I give you all of me.

The gratitude I feel for your kindness
And thoughtfulness gives wings to my heart.
A hawk, a dove, an eagle, a swan
What wings strong yet gentle,
Eyes sharp yet soft.

I feel your soul vibration.
My soul breathes with the gentle
Essence of your soul.

It is light. It is light.
You are a radiant breath of air so sweet.
I am nurtured by your light.
I am more alive.

Your voice carries me to happiness.
When I hear it, I return to heaven,
The realm of light.
There's a melody in your words.
When you talk to me you are
Always singing a song.

You inspire me to create,
To shape out of nothing, something
And because of you it is good;
It is beautiful;
It speaks the truth
Without saying a word.

Your wellbeing is my concern
I watch out for you in time.
No one can harm you
While I am present.
I take care of your soul with you.
My love for you is a shield of light.
My eyes sparkle with awareness
Because you're near.

Occasionally we even touch
On the physical plane,
A loving touch,
A friendly hug,

A synchronistic closeness of our bodies.
The memory of that lighted exchange
Stays with me.
I savor the blessing.
My whole being is touched.

Sometimes my heart is on fire
Like a mighty sun.
I feel a cool heat
Filling the spaces
Between the atoms and molecules
Of my body.
Your presence fans the fire.
It is a conscious nuclear fire
Which lights our space.

We share a common purpose.
It is a miracle;
It is magic.
People are changed,
We are transformed.
We are butterflies soaring on a warm breeze.
Others see our colorful wings
And begin creating their silken cocoons.

Our children are calling.
We have many children
All over the world.
They are crying for help.
They are hungry for light,
For unconditional love,
For the wisdom of ancient souls.

We are making toys of joy
To give them.
Their souls will play in a pool of light,
Golden liquid light.
They will remember
And they will share their joy.

You are the mother of these children of light.
You love them and nurture them.
We join souls alchemically.
Our essences become a beacon of light
For our children.
Before, the night had no moon or stars.
Now they see.
Our light lights their light.
Before long the night will have endless stars,
A moon and even a sun at dawn.

Let's light candles,
Burn incense
And listen to the music of the spheres.
Let's meditate together
Focusing our energies on the field of dreams.
Bright images are gifts from angels.
These creative ideas are the blueprints
For our children's happiness.
There's a lot of playful
Work ahead of us.

Our love generates a warm wind
From the south.

Our bellies are full of life.
We are laughing our way to
Enlightenment.
Our bellies ache with laughter
That ache is the movement of light
Into our bellies.
We cry tears of happiness.
Each happy tear is the magic potion
Taken by suffering souls to heal their agony.

Each morning I experience
Your light and special love.
Your mental clarity refocuses my mind.
Your spirit energizes my soul.
Your loving heart reminds me
I'm not alone.
Your beauty transmutes
Darkness into light.
The shadows of my soul
Are illuminated by your bright smile
And clear blue eyes.

Sometimes angels whisper in my ears.
They tell me wonderful things about you.
Your wisdom, your knowing, your loving,
They tell me you carry a special purpose
In your heart which you share with
Family, friends, me, and many
Others around the world.

They tell me you are a great woman
With diamond light in your aura.

Many are blinded by your radiance.
They are fearful and run away.
Others, who are ready,
Drink the goddess nectar
That you pour from your heart.
I love to drink your light.
It quenches my thirst
After crossing the desert all day.
I am deeply grateful for your light.
I give you my love in whatever
Form you need it,
Whenever you need it.

The angels tell me there's
A powerful love near.
Your time of loneliness is neatly over.
You passed through the fire.
You were ashes.
Out of the white smoke
Your spirit stirred
And swirled and took shape.

Your angel wings spread
You flew into the light.
You remembered the ancient wisdom.
Light beings became your friends
And you felt heaven on earth.

They tell me much about your greatness.
I have the privilege of being
One of the guardians of the treasure.
The gold, silver, diamonds, and jewels

That you have brought with you
Make you wealthy
Beyond the wildest dreams.

No one will steal the treasure
As long as I'm a guardian.
You will share your riches
When the time is right.
Until then, I stand watch day and night –
Vigilant, keen, eagle-eyed.

My love for you is mighty.
It surrounds you and
Your soul's treasure gently
Yet with the strength of a god
Whose will has been tempered
On the battlefields of
A thousand incarnations.

When you think of me
I appear.
When you need me
I come.
When you are in danger
I arrive
With my light sword drawn.

You are truly a Woman of Light
Who has grounded her light on earth.
I love you forever
Which is eternally now.
We share everything.

What is mine is yours.
I give you all of me.

Man of Light

The Man of Light travels through time
Yet remains nowhere in everything.
This is the riddle that has no reason or rhyme.
Yet is solved by following the spiral string.

There are many a galactic mountain he must climb
Before he learns the lesson of a cosmic king
Solves the riddle and finds the ring in time
Before the cosmic dragon delivers his sting.

The Man of Light is born a titan star,
A Red Giant in a rage of desire
Exploding arms of fire out afar
Into fields of black motion and mire.

Within his raging body shines a star,
A silent glowing white dwarf light,
A dancing note on a harmonic bar
Ringing a soundless sound into a dark night.

Within this dancing dwarf rests the Androgynous One,
A neutron star, a glowless glow
Concealing the answer to the cosmic pun
Hidden inside untold eons ago.

Mysteriously within, nothing, a black hole
Full of no light, no matter, no sound,
The forever concealed galactic soul,
A rotating infinity unbound, unfound.

The Man of Light has made the circuit complete
Solved the riddle of time-space
And become a Cosmic King with infinity at his feet
And a golden spiral dancing before his face.

Man, Virgin and Son

A vast ocean of space motion
Etheric substance giving birth to form
Comes also the mysterious mercurial potion.

The Virgin of Light in supple form
Gathers in a golden vase this sacred oil
That emanates through space, the cosmic soil
Suppling the soul with strength to transform.

When her vase is full of magic emptiness
She brings it to the Man of Light
Sleeping on a galactic cloud at night
And washes his head and hands with happiness.

Aware of her presence as essence
The Man awakens a new vibration
Of sound and color within his cosmic nation
And opens his golden liquid eyes from nescience.

Arising from his swirling cloud bed
A deep booming voice in perfect tone
Bellows 'ECCE HOMO" through an etheric cone
While the Man and the Virgin whirl in dread.

Then in silence they merged together
And passed through each other and dissolved
And emerged, calm, peaceful and resolved
Of the dread, knowing it was the voice of the Father.

They probed with their minds
Great galaxies of time
Until they touched the ringing chime
Of planetary bells, earth, and mankind.

Now the Man knew what he must do
Descend the spiral course to earth reality
And experience again physical mortality
To test his godhood, the beautiful and the true.

The Virgin of Light kissed him goodbye
With a golden ray from her heart
As the Man spun downward like a fiery dart
Farther into matter his light to crucify.

An agonizing birth as an infant child
To find himself in the forbidden realm
Crying from the pain that overwhelms
And the desire that makes his flesh run wild.

A father, a mother provides for their son
Feed him love, faith, understanding and hope

Powerful forces to mold the coming one
An avatar with a blessed horoscope.

For seven years the boy grows and learns
He studies the tree, the river, the earth
He watches the flight of birds and yearns
For the regions of space motion before birth.

The age of twelve, a total cycle complete
He speaks of knowledge unheard
By men considered to be wise and discrete
Worlds of vast regions of beauty superb.

As the Man's earth life spirals on
He gathers disciples from every land
To learn of physical and spiritual phenomena
Not from words and speech but firsthand.

"Experience is the seed of Wisdom,"
Spoke the Man of Light to those around him
Then pointing to the great sky-dome
He sang a hymn to the seraphim.

"Awaken my memory of the Virgin
Wonderous winged beings on high
So, she can help me begin
The return journey to regions beyond the sky.

For thirty years in this far realm
Have I been beaten and torn
Until I can no longer be overwhelmed
So now awaken my memory this golden morn."

Three times the Man did sing this song
Till glorious angels filled the sky-dome
To listen to the voice of one of the strong
And help him return to his sacred home.

Ecstatic vibrations of joy filled the air
Until its pitch lifted him upward
Into the sky-dome above the despair
Of earth reality that the Man abhorred.

At last, before him through the vast ocean
Of space motion came the Virgin of Light
Carrying in her arms their Christos Son
The Three – Man, Virgin and Son did unite.

1000 Petaled Lotus – Dr. G for Jhene Aiko

Incarnates with Star Consciousness
Limitless Love and Light
Soon meets with
Resistance, challenges,
Problems and darkness,
The leading edge of learning
And the expansion
Of consciousness
Let the fireworks begin
It's the 4th of July and
New Years combined
Increases in Light and Love
By embracing a

Renewed focus
The beast is beauty
In disguise
Awaken, Transform.

The Way of Wisdom 1

Function faithfully day by day
So, the forces of your being
Become balanced along the way
To Light, Love, Wisdom, Seeing.

Meditate consciously on the moment
Not on the past or future
This is the true covenant
Between human and Jupiter.

Walk and talk with awareness
The shining armor of the soul
Lest you fall into the darkness
Of a deep forbidding hole.

Structure your every action
The masonry of a Coming One
Chaos and confusion, he cannot sanction
Brick by brick his work is done.

Set a rhythm to your life
In daily sweat and play
It will take away the strife
And tune you to your inner ray.

The Way of Wisdom 2

Wisdom's way is hard
So, step lightly
At times be the bard
Sing a song nightly.

Wisdom's way is lonely
So, spend time with others
You are not the only
Somewhere there are brothers.

Wisdom's way is long
So, take your time
Make yourself strong
Before you begin the climb.

Wisdom's way is slow
So, become patient
Then you will surely grow
While making the ascent.

Wisdom's way is painful
So, seek out pleasure
Not that of the fool
But consciously at your leisure.

The Way of Wisdom 3

Positive, Negative, Neutral
The forces of creation
In head, foot and entrail
Continually in transformation.

Rajas, Tamas, Sattva
The three-fold substance
Known by every Mahatma
To comprise the Cosmic Dance.

Knowledge, Love, Understanding
In proper proportion
A triangular fire burning
In the heart of every nation.

Thought, Feeling, Action
The tools of daily life
To build a healthy station
Against all sickness and strife.

Structure, Function, Order
The weapons against delusion
Not used, life is harder
Used there is no illusion.

The Way of Wisdom 4

When you're weary on the way
Relax, take things day by day.
Focused relaxation is the key
To true rest as you be.

Work with effort to overcome
The negative crud and scum
Then time and eternity
Will merge eventually.

As you walk, be aware
This will take away every care.
Tune the eye to see
The forces that be.

When you awake each day
Get in the body right away.
Don't let the mind wander
At other times it's right to ponder.

Make your ideas fit the fact
Any other way shows lack of tact.
Senses come before mind
Otherwise, life's a double-bind.

The Way of Wisdom 5

Space-time, energy-matter
Blended and balanced each hour
Help us climb the stellar ladder
Toward the light of wise power.

North-south, east-west
The gods of the four directions
Face each other and pass the test
Then make your Noetic connections.

Hear-see, taste-smell
These senses use
They tell of heaven and hell
Then touch what you choose.

Force-form, field-function
Use consciously to build
An inter-galactic conjunction
The Love and Wisdom filled.

Earth-water, fire-air
Bring the soul vitality
Through psychic weather foul and fair
Together they form reality.

The Way of Wisdom 6

Plant your feet on the earth
To study the natural process
This leads to the second birth
And away from carnal excess.

Observe your thoughts and feeling
Study their every turn
This will bring you healings
And greater things to learn.

Balance head, heart, and hand
Through each cycle
This leads to the promised land
Guarded by the archangel Michael.

Learn to reason clearly
In physics and geometry
Then Wisdom loves you dearly
As you climb the Cosmic Tree.

Measure every word you say
It's a matter of life and death
This is Wisdom's way
To a deeper rhythmic breath.

Do What Must Be Done

But Never More than Needed
Do not go too far
In any one direction
Then your inner fire
Will never face extinction

Do what must be done
But never more than needed
Then the inner fire
Will not be overheated.

Measure each step taken
Morning, noon, and night
Lest you be forsaken
By the ever-present light.

Use the eyes, the mind
To see what must be done
Then you're sure to find
Your inner shining one.

Balance is an art
Practice day by day
It leads to the golden heart
This is Wisdom's way.

The Seven Windows

In the head there are seven windows
Opening to a multi-celled mind, the eighth
And I am the ninth of those
The Man of Light come to regenerate.

Seven windows have each a frame,
Four sides to a frame are twenty-eight.
Seven steps in four directions to regain
The lost light Man needs to illuminate.

Seven windows of multi-luminous hue,
Rose red the left eye,
Orpheus orange the right, make two
Glowing panes of glass that glorify.

Seven windows of multi-luminous hue
Yoga yellow the left of the nose
Beatrice blue the right, make two
Glowing panes of glass in equipoise.

Seven windows of multi-luminous hue
Isis indigo the left ear
Vishnu violet the right, make two
Glowing panes of glass that hear.

Seven windows of multi-luminous hue
Grail green the mouth,
The seventh glowing pane of glass through
Which flow the energies of growth.

The mind is a multi-celled window ablaze
Seeing through a seven windowed head
The Man of Light racing through space
Revealing everything, leaving nothing unsaid.

Text Poem 1: Midnight 2013

Presents fall like snowflakes
On frozen cornfields.
Souls fill like silos
At harvest time.
Light your fireplace heart.
Time melts at 32 degrees.
May happiness play
In your loving soul
From dawn till
Midnight 2013.

Text Poem 2: Murky

No snow.
The city is awful murky.
So strange.
Murky fills my heart
With mist or fog.
Too warm to feel snow
Except on the farm
In winter.
Or in the barn

In summer.
Silos empty.
The country is murky.
Snowless awful,
The city with no snow
At Christmas.

Text Poem 3: Mother Buzz

Bumble Bee, the buzz.
Bees taste flowers.
More Buzz,
Away from the Hive House.
Got some nectar
In the bee buzz.
Flowered yellow like the Sun.
Now the Sun,
That's one mighty buzz.
The Mother of all Bees.
Got some Sun nectar
For Mother Bee.
Mother buzz in the Hive House

Text Poem 4: Black Ice

Snow and ice, 25 degrees.
Can't drive on black ice.
Lagunitas cappuccino stout.
Roses used to be red.

Violets were never blue.
Why turn the corner?
I like being a corner.
Keeps me sharp.
But not sharp as a tack.
Slipping on snow and ice
Requires some acrobatics
And a swig of stout.
Black ice is the swirling gateway
To a deep space black hole.

Text Poem 5: Fluid

Easing in and out,
Fluid feelings,
Tides of thought motion.
Energy space stars
And light waves.
Splash across galaxies.
What time do you have?
Tell me without looking
At a clock or smartphone.
Please don't think about it;
Just tell me; say it.
I felt the splash of time
On the beach of space.
Everything is on schedule
And at ease.
Fluid.

Text Poem 6: Play for Fun

Flying over and under
And the space within without.
Stop thinking for …
Time Gap. Happy?
I'd rather be serene in a conscious way.
Stay with me here.
Make sense of whatever you want.
Coming in for a landing.
Earth to air.
Stopping for half a …
On my way.
You're on your way.
Play for fun. What else?
Smile.

Text Poem 7: On the Eve of Your Last Day on Earth

Time is a smooth current
Washing up and over life.
Leaving behind traces of innocence.
Hiding the truth or
Revealing the pain.
Always flowing, seeking,
Altering its path.
Until the day the moon is high
And its reflection, motionless
On the eve of your last day on earth.

As the last breath passes your lips,
You're now one with the water
That once lapped your feet.
The time has passed to care
Or worry or fret.
You are free to ride high
And sing in the space
Full of peace.

Text Poem 8: Question Marks & Explanation Points

Soaring question marks
Turn into red balloons
100 miles across.
Riding the question
To an answer that's
Really an explanation point.
Planning not to plan.
The moment is a red balloon
No bigger than a point.
Or dot, or Hindu Bindu.
Playing ping pong
With time waves.
Playing croquet
With questions marks
And explanation points.
Skip to your Lou my darling.
Wink.

Text Poem 9: My Garage is a Music Store

My garage is a music store.
Bargain for the clang of hubcaps
And detuned engines
Throwing pistons into orbit
Around the sun.
Hear the sound
Of rakes and shovels
In my music garage.
Recording a garage album.
Apple iTunes said no.
Iceland plays it day and night.
What night?
There's a hammer in my music garage
That plays one note.
Hammer, hammer.
Screwdriver and pliers.
Maybe that's three notes.

Text Poem 10: Imported from Outer Space

Imported from outer space.
Imports are not cheap.
I'll buy that star stuff
No matter the price.
From churn to turn
Spirals on the brain.
I gave up thinking

For vegetables and bread.
Happiness. What?
Stop that line, circle,
And spiral of thought.
Imported from space.
I'm at the dock
Ready for an import-ant.
Winding through a mind twist
Importing myself
From star stuff.

Text Poem 11

Sipping hot water with
Fresh squeezed lemon
While home alone
Together
Experiencing a
Biological tsunami.
Grateful to be home free
Outside there's winter
Weather.
I'm far from being done.
Patience waiting for a
New sun
Aging father, mother,
Brother
Sipping organic green tea.

Text Poem 12

Open mind,
Lungs full of air
Piercing the heart barrier,
Faster than the speed of love.
At three times the speed of love
You enter the Wisdom zone.
No twilight, only light
And a cup of espresso.
Smooth flow of tender thoughts
And the soft warm glow
Of deep human connection.
Dinner is served.
A hug is on the menu
And not just for dessert.
Why wear your heart
On your sleeve.
That's too breakfast
At Tiffany.
Wisdom has more heart
Than black hole adrenaline love.
What's for dinner?

Something for the heart please.
I'll go with dark chocolate
And chills
Up and down the spine.

Text Poem 13

Dynamic strings resonate
Notes, chords
And winged feelings.
Listen, listen.
Thoughts soar as songbirds
Swiftly play.
Heart song,
The only song that
Lives forever.
Ever richly melodic
Whispering in silent shouts
At the top of roofs
Near the eagles.
Glide in warm wind.
Gently touching the string,
A feeling blossoms
Across space-time.
Stars embrace the music
Of the soul.
Listen to it.
Listen with a soft ear.
Hearing it is magnificence.

Text Poem 14

Spiraling colors emerald and turquoise
Spin a path.
Follow the neon light,

Electric cool.
Follow the feeling
Speaking silent in a heart
Of Golden light.
Sink into the wakeful peace
Alert and alive.
This path has no direction
But taking it leads to your
True home.
Sweet home emanating
Emerald and turquoise
Universes sprinkled with star play.
This is the way of not wanting
Or grasping.
It's special without being important.
You're invited by the divine presence
To breathe, feel color,

Text Poem 15

A rainbow-winged hawk
Swooped passed
Gliding then lifting
Toward red and orange leaves.
Messenger with a strong
And long wingspan
Hints at new opportunities
In the air.
An inner smile lights caves
Of river thoughts
And ocean wave feelings.

Knowing change and choice
Makes the hawk a friend
Whispering with the
Flap of color and feather.
The eyes are energy
Looking with magic
And mysterious wisdom love.
The gifts show themselves.
The hawk tells me to just
Open them and let
Surprise wash across the spine.

Text Poem 16

Red ink surges through this pen
Like a flash flood.
Earthy iron crimson pain
And the sizzle of cuts.
Soon hopes and dreams
And fears will be forgotten.
Only red will continue
Bleeding in a spectrum of reds.
Knives and flowing blood.
Watch it dry on the cut.
The pen moves slicing
Red ink through words that
Bleed on paper napkins.
Scratch paper.
Blood stains, not words.
The alphabet of reds.
Red ink, red pen, blood.

Bleeding, iron ore, steel.
Fire, hot, white fire.
Words and pen on fire.
Red ink burns the skin
On the writing hand,
Sizzling in blood.

Text Poem 17

Bison pie
It makes me hi
Smoke it, coke it
Rock it.
Shot the bison
With my smoke
And mirrors.
Cloaked my bison
Brain.
Ninja invisibility. I
Don't even know it
Or see it. Feel it.
African tree in a
Forest.
Smoke that
Buffalo.

Text Poem 18

The familiar,
Habitual,
Attached, likes, dislikes,
End years, 70, what
I'm used to,
Adverse to
Change, the way
It is comfort
Zone, couch
Potatoes.

Text Poem 19

See the light in the dark
Ride the sun ark
Awareness is light
Use it thru the night
It's a gift we often forget
An eternal brilliant sunset.

Text Poem 20

The sweet notes in your
Poetry touches my inner melody.
Jamie, you sing the words in
Harmonic combination

In soundless whispers and
Thoughtful fun.

Text Poem 21

Everything orbits
Around everything.
Galaxies and atoms and stars.
All sing in an eternal choir
Of light music.
Strum your mind,
Body, soul strings.
The song of continuous
Creating. Bring your
Mental focus to the task
At hand.
Feel the light
Waves flow like ocean
Currents in space.
Time boils away in a puff of steam.
Welcome to the happiness dream.

Text Poem 22

The color of light
Soars like wind
Upward to the
World of light.
What I am

And you are
And we are.
Profound Love-Light.
An opportunity
For samsara liberation
From the round
Of attachments
And endless
Identification with greed
Consumer things
And ego's
False security.
Play in the
Non-attachment of sand, water
And endless thinking.
I bow to the now
Feeling the wow
Of Tao
Light piercing
The eye of I.

Text Poem 23

Go to the Greek Islands.
Sip wine at Tahoe.
Play tennis in the rain.
The joints spin
Money wheels.
Black holes of green.
The dealer deals
The heart of a queen.

Text Poem 24

The winter of discontent
The sun's rays prism bent.
Eastward winds devour
The sun.
Night before the day is done.

Text Poem 25

Pool ocean beach.
Toward the future reach.
No work, no play
Only peace inside
Each day.

Text Poem 26

It can be the dead of winter
And the summer sun keeps
Me warm inside and out.
I felt a big problem capture my mind
And stick the crazy glue to my emotions.
At first, the sun started setting
In my August and December.
I'm warm inside
Even when the sun sets outside.

In a lucid dream
I traveled into the realm of light
And waved to a rainbow feathered bird
Who waved back.
Heavy drama is winter in summer,
Fall in spring.
The heart smiles no matter what.
That's freedom of religion.

Text Poem 27

The twisted DNA bursts to the sucking
Of lemon drops.
What's a pucker?
Lemon drops and DNA.
That's a true pucker.
How sour and DNA lemony sweet.
I put the last lemon in the freezer.
Frozen, I took it out
And grated it on a Greek salad with olives.
Olives and lemons.
My DNA spirals for this taste.
Let's travel to a lemon world
Of bright solar yellow.
Turns your DNA
Into non-biological love.
How sourly sweet.
Mmmmmmmmm.

Text Poem 28

Looking with magic and mysterious wisdom love.
The gifts show themselves.
The hawk tells me to jut open them
And let surprise wash
Across the spine.

Text Poem 29

Spiraling colors emerald and turquoise
Spin a path.
Follow the neon light
Electric cool.
Follow the feeling
Speaking silent in a heart
Of golden light.
Sink into the wakeful peace
Alert and alive.
This path has no direction
But taking it leads to
Your true home
Sweet home
Emanating emerald
And turquoise universes
Sprinkled with star dust.
This is the way
Of not wanting or grasping.
It's special
Without being important.

You're invited by the divine
Presence to breath,
Feel color,
And taste the sweet light.

Junk Mail 1

Visa Slavery
Enter the credit temple
Chained to just 19.8,
A web of plastic cash.
Apply today
Before it's stolen from the trash.

Sign on the dotted line,
No annual fee.
Join Visa slavery,
Neo-Plantation Capitalism,

Pass through the pearly gate,
You'll have hell to pay.
Don't delay; apply today,
Chained to just 19.8.

Junk Mail 2

Spy Hard Drive
007 in your hard drive,
Die another freedom please

Monitor your children,
Husband, wife, and employees.

Spying, lying software
Big sister, big brother 1984.
Every email you send
Every website memory you store.

Watching without you knowing
Stealing your privacy
Spy software solutions,
Generating soul pollutions.

Junk Mail 3

AARP
90-day money back guarantee
Temporary membership card
For roadside assistance call toll free.

Retired people motoring plan
This is not a credit card
Will bill you later

AARP
Sign, agree
Call toll free

Junk Mail 4

Akashic Record 33 1/3
The akashic record 33 1/3
Spiritual growth and development CD
Dear Dr. Nielsen
Sincerely, Isabelle.

"Tranquil and serene must I be
To allow all that is mine to come to me."
Escape reality, face reality
Paint the face,
Cosmic embrace.
Affirmation, confirmation,
Imprinting the world soul.

Zaccardi, Ph.D. tranquility
July 22, 2002, like a good friend,
It is always there when needed.
San Rafael, archangel air,

Feeling safe re-grouping
Serene, tranquil, peaceful.
Dear Dr. Nielsen
Sincerely, Isabelle Zaccardi.

Trapeze Act: Esther, 21

Twenty point nine, nine, nine
Twenty-one.

Legalese on the flying trapeze.
Big top vision, surgeon eyes
Burning through buy now, pay later.
A sixty second burger war
And a thirty-year fixed.

Swinging between curse and blessing.
Esther with her scalpel ball-point
Flying across the page
Mightier than the sword.

A woman writing the edge
Taking her act on the road
To Wall Street, Main Street
And Madison Avenue.

The Akashic Record 33 1/3

A single 45
Spiritual growth and development CD
Dear Dr. Nielsen
Sincerely, Isabelle.
"Tranquil and serene must I be
To allow all that is mine to come to me."
Escape reality, face reality
Paint the face,
Cosmetic embrace
Affirmation, confirmation
Imprinting the world soul.
Zaccardi, PhD tranquility.
July 22, 2002, like a good friend.

It is always there when needed
San Rafael, Archangel of Air
Feeling safe, re-grouping
Serene, tranquil, peaceful
Dear Dr. Nielsen
Sincerely, Isabelle Zaccardi.

Earthwalk 1

Calm the thought, feeling, action boil
Plant your life seed in perception's soil.
Awareness of positive-negative brings light
To mind-body, guiding star in blackest night.

The animal in man hungers, desires
Roasts and burns in hell's fires
Cool your urges, your wants, your cravings
Take careful note of how you're behaving.

Lower emotion wants to rule the roost
Give the orders, avoid structure's boost.
You must take charge, be the boss
Otherwise, a lighted life is your loss.

Heated speech is automatic mutter
By the higher considered deluded stutter.
Keep the word plain and sane
Unemotional, devoid of suffering and pain.

Do not run around helter-skelter
Your energy level is your shelter.

Make your actions ordered, measured
That will bring what you have treasured.

Lords of Light

Lords of Light
Set me on the path
Shine through the night.
Transform the shadow's wrath.
I ask from my heart
To receive the call
I want to do my part
To remove the wall
That separates the soul
From the god-source
That makes us whole
And activates the force.
Enter the Temple
The Natural order is my temple.
Light is my golden blood.
My consciousness is a rising star.
My thoughts are musical notes.
My breaths are rhythmic spirit
My mind is a time-traveler.
My body is space
Structured with bone.
My arms and legs are
4th dimensional spiral wheels
Whirling, unfurling
Curling, hurling.
A voided light spray

Of ego sacrifice pray.
Enter the temple today.
Shed the golden blood
Catch a rising star
Sing your thoughts
Feel the space-time joy song.

Laws of Growth

Know when you plant
The seeds of feeling and thought
That you'll reap what you've sought
Regardless of your rave or rant.

Know your subconscious soil
Is it rocky, sandy or loam
Its quality attracts your home
Even though you boil and toil.

To grow organically
Both day and night
Sharpen your insight
And do everything rhythmically.

Tend the soul's garden
Of structures, functions, orders
Keep weed delusions from its borders
And yourself you'll never pardon.

Water the seeds of knowledge
With the water of attention

It takes constant repetition
To grow out of the mire and sledge.

Light Pyramid

Light-Man emanates pattern
Glowing colored pyramids and spheres
The toil and test of Saturn
Thought forms reflected in cosmic mirrors.

Scintillating green, rays of red
Permeate his golden auric field
Rotating, transmuting the earthly lead
Into gold light-point-seeds well sealed.

A spiraling ray leaves the center
Of the Light-Man's head
Travels its measured course to enter
An orbiting thought-form and wed

Consciousness to form, birthing anew
Being – A son born of his essence
A third from the two,
The growth of a universal intelligence.

Little light-pyramid-son orbits
An entire galaxy of mind-rays
Heart-suns and foot-planets
Searching through a galactic maze.

For the Light-Man source
And the Mother form
With a powerful mind-heart force
Probing, scanning, getting warm,

A simple vision of his body-structure
Awakens a memory of his mother pattern
Within which resides a consciousness pure,
The Light-Man-Field, the source, the return.

Swirling Force

Troubled swirl of force can dismay
The walker of the straight and narrow way.
Negative thought-feeling energy field
The master of force will bend and yield.

Swirling force all men receive
Store, radiate till they finally achieve
Control of thought, feeling, will
No more to rape, steal or kill.

Positive force awakens, enlightens
Cleanses, purifies, and brightens
The energy-force-field soul
To make the raiment body whole.

Positive, negative, neutral, three-fold force
Triangular form on a spiral course
Focused in multi-ordinal structured points
Vibrating in body, bone, and joints.

Force in atoms, molecules, and cells,
Energy to cross the ignorant's hells
Precious life-essence use wisely
Don't waste or spill, be miserly.

Star-Field

Rotating force-field of coiled energy
Pulsating positive-negative light.
Alternating emanation joy-mystery,
What a seer sees clairvoyant sight.

Moving, standing not there,
A living structured soul
Built of earth, water, fire, air,
The ark of mind ordered-whole.

Sailing an ocean of subtle currents
Of sound-color and invisible waves
The silent marriage of our cosmic parents,
In the adytum of 1000 caves.

In the distance spiraling snowflakes
Each another hexagonal star-seed
Planted in the cosmic substance that makes
Through process of growth stars to feed.

The hungry mind-soul-boat
Sails through a star-field
Balanced, tuned, constantly afloat

Eating gratefully another cycle's yield.
Consciousness

Conscious structured point many-eyed
Penetrating the earth's crusty hide
Bringing sight to deep caves,
Spaces between atomic waves.

Electron-planets in spiral orbit
Inner space stations silently lit
By Sun-protons and microscope eyes
Tiny solar system lives --- dies.

Geo-logic engrams in rock crystal
Unspeakable memories digest in earth entrails
The minds of Light-Men-Women find tuned
See the answers plainly runed.

Beside the quiet waters of nuclear seas
Balanced beings awaken from a deep freeze
Here the call of transmitting souls
And leave electron-planets thru black holes.

Wombs of earthly energy-mothers
Giving birth to energy world brothers
Who bring gifts of organic science,
Natural order process, and new age alliance.

Cosmic Code

Light waves travel nowhere
Are everywhere;
Sense the vibrations
Through time-space
And the human race.
Be the light
You are,
A cosmic star.
Time standing still,
Clocks stop,
Stand on top
Of the world.
In the source,
The universal force.
Be the light being,
Limitless seeing
Through people, places, things
Till every cell sings
A chorus of harmony;
Mind-body unite,
Day-night light.

Cosmic Evolution

Sand, stone, and rock
Nature's mineral clock
Crystal structures six and eight
Reflects the universal state.

Flower, bush, and tree
Plants are all three
Transforming light to substance
An alchemical sun-moon dance.

Fish, reptile, and mammal
All three are animal
Instinctive movement each
The higher they aspire to reach.

Man-Woman has all three
Plus, he-she can see
Think, be and know
Thus, can consciously grow.

Grow into more than man
If he-she follows the true plan
Cosmic structure, function, order
Will take you beyond life's border.

Where There's a Will ...
Suffering, strife, and toil
To overcome emotion's boil
Steady your mind-body, two in one
And in your heart will be born a golden sun.

Difficulties, hardships, pain
Will eventually make you sane
No matter what you think and say
It's what you do day today.

Sickness, disease, death
Take away the balanced breath
Focused relaxation is a mighty key
Practiced it will set you free.

Darkness, danger, fright
Puts out every higher light
Be conscious of every motion
That's the secret life-giving potion.

Hate, greed, and pride
Toughens loves soft side
Kill these mighty beasts
A sacrifice to wise priests.

A Tablespoon of Vomit

The giving gone out of Thanksgiving.
Stuffed myself instead of the turkey.
Repulsive acid reflux,
A tablespoon of vomit
Erupts to an unreceptive mouth.

I washed it down with a bad
California Merlot.
I don't feel any gratitude,
Thinking about how bad I have it.

Loved the hot spinach dip
And garlic bread.
Guess I'm grateful for that.

Actors, directors, and Ph.Ds.
Blowing smoke, puffing, huffing
Stuffing myself with an aching stomach.

Gorging myself with ingratitude
And pumpkin pie.
Washing it all down with French toast.

Home Farm – Baker, Nevada - Summer 1991

To The School of the Natural Order
On the Nevada/Utah border:
Dane and I thank you for our time
Experiencing Home Farm's rhythm & rhyme.

We loved our days of rest & play,
To begin to feel our Cosmic Ray.
We are grateful to *The Field*,
A mighty love-light shield.

We loved our daily meditation,
To drink the light-field libation.
The I Am, is the Power
Which we are Conscious of hour by hour.

Chanting the AUM tuned our souls
To the Omnipresent, multidimensional whole.
In the name of the Father, Mother, Son
The infinite triangle, the three that are one.

Thank you for the food at eight and five
That kept our physical vehicles alive.
Sitting 'round the tables sharing
Feeling the Home Farm family caring.

Dane and I miss you all.
Home Farm is our favorite port of call.
We look forward to our return;
There's so much more to learn.

Costa Rican Turtle

Tropical time is a turtle
Swimming and walking.
A sea breeze sweeps
Grains of sand into dust.
Thoughts have translucent sails
Filled with tranquility,
Sailing the Gulf of Nicoya.
The turtle paddles
With gliding strokes,
Walks with patient feet.
Trees and flowers
Stretch touching the sun.
Fish breath the salt.
Tropical time ticks
Every one-hundred years
Like the turtle's heart.

Tortuga de Puntarenas

El tiempo tropical es una torguga
El nadar y el caminar.
Barridos de una brisa de mar
Granos de arena en el polvo.
Los pensamientos tienen velas translucidias
Llenadas de tranquillidad,
Navegando el Golfo de Nicoya.
Las paletas de la Tortuga
Con los movimientos de deslizamiento
Caminatas con las pies pacientes
Arboles y flores
Estiramiento que toca el sol.
Respiracion de los peces respiran
Senales tropicales del tiempo
Cada cien anos
Como el corzaon de los tortugas.

Para Miquel, Iris, Felix, Jenni, Lianna, Winnie and El
Loro

Dating

Mating, dating, love connection
Day or night, day, and night
I've been dating for forty years
Nothing but fears and tears
Desiring the biochemical
Hand of fate

Crazy glue bonding
Wedding bell hell
I've told my story
Until it makes me sick
To my stomach
How many people have fallen
In love to find out they
Hate each other?
Fallen, crashed out of love
Sweep her off her feet
Forget it
Here's a broom and a dustpan
Sweep yourself off your own feet
Rock your world
Buy yourself a rocking chair
And rock your own world
My last date was with a married
Woman, her husband was out of town.
The date before that was with
A woman getting married
In the summer.
A couple months ago
I went to a party
Met a woman I tried to
Ask out years ago
She would not give me the time of day
She forgot that time
Now she gave me her number
I almost called but I decided
Not to give her the time of day
I went to a housewarming party
Last Sunday

I met someone I wanted
To meet for years
There I was actually having a
Conversation with her
Hundreds of times my mind
Has locked hearts
With someone I felt was special
Now I can't even remember
Their names
If I can't even remember
Their names
If I get to know this new woman
Will I remember her name?
A few months from now?
I'm not looking for mad love
I'm looking for a companion
To share love without going mad.
Last winter I met a woman
Through work
That week she was fired
Not because of me
But because she was late a lot
And drinking too much.
On our first date she fell
Down drunk on the dance floor
She called a few days later
Asking to meet for coffee
The next morning
I waited. She never showed up
Later she called telling me
How sorry she was for
Forgetting

I guess it was pretty obvious
We would never get together
Till death do us part.
Around my birthday last year
My best friends encouraged
Me to go out with a woman
They thought would be good for me
She told me how much she cared
About me and then I never
Heard from her again.
A month later I heard she tried
To commit suicide.
I tried to call her numerous times
To have an open conversation
You know, to communicate
She never returned any of my calls
I bumped into her one day
She was superficially friendly
She acted like nothing ever happened.

Dream Images

Open window escape
Invisible walls.
How old are you?
I tell her 45
You look 26
She likes I'm wearing plaid.
Facing hypnotic force
Shake tree
Female squirrel

Exposed too much sun
Turned red
Cleaned my closet.
One hundred-year trees uproot crashing
Avalanche of trees
Running a red light
Ancient box
Blue helix veins torso
Mt. Shasta erupts
Ash rain burns arms / legs
Boat Lake Minnetonka.

Dishwasher Sounds Like the Staten Island Ferry

Your dishwasher sounds like
The Staten Island Ferry.
I heard footsteps in the fog
While listening to the
Down Syndrome Girls,
An all-girl band.
I took a drink
Of gritty tap water
And washed it down with
A Jack and Coke.
Your dishwasher sounds like
The Staten Island Ferry.
I was hungry for a
White trash casserole.
I asked my elbowologist

To tickle my funny bone
And tell me
Who gives good brain
She told me not to go
Out with women who worked
For the CIA.
Your dishwasher sounds like
The Staten Island Ferry.
I snacked on Rocky Mountain Oysters,
Sheep testicles if you didn't know,
And octopus pancakes.
It was the end of April
And I just turned on the heat
When her soft breast
Pressed my receptive bicep.

Gone Hollywood

Wrote a screenplay
Called *Selling Out*,
Gone Hollywood.

Box office blockbuster,
Option, contract, residuals
Writer's jackpot,
Malibu beach house.

Selling Out is about
A guy who pretends
To believe in God.
Gone Hollywood.

His pretending is so believable
Others follow him,
Hang on his every word.
He knows he doesn't know,
Knows he's Gone Hollywood.

Producers, directors, movie stars.
Premier, limo, champagne,
Good guy, bad guy,
Gone Hollywood.

The bigger the lie
The happier the happy ending.
Selling Out nominated
For best picture.
Oscar, Gone Hollywood.

Selling Out is up against
A thriller, a comedy,
A sci-fi and a western.
Selling Out is a hybrid comedy
horror film.
Gone Hollywood.

Home

I long for a home
My own place,
Space.
Where silence

Is golden
Light.
A home
My very own
Home.
A place to dream,
To write,
Play music
And talk freely
With friends.
Having a home
Feels good
Not having a home
Feels bad.
I long for a home,
My own place.

Friendship

Your friendship means so much
Warms a heart from balanced touch
To see your lovable smile
Eases daily toil's trial.

Your kindness is boundless giving
Can make the weary go on living
Brings a bit of joy to life
And lifts the weight of constant strife.

Your energy so sweet and light
Frees a soul from earth bound light

From earth to star and back
A quality most others lack.

A perception pointed and true
Most things do not escape you
When you tell of what you see
Others cannot help but agree.

Playful and fun loving at times
Eternal child in a woman's mimes
Laughing and frolicking each day
Comic relief in life's real play.

Where did you come from my friend?
Not from where most descend
For your heart is living love
Radiated from source above.

Flip the Switch

Energy zaps space
Disappearing face
Stretch the mind
The spirit find.

Energy flowing
Eyes glowing
Flip the soul
Give it a roll.

Turning into light
Illumines night
Lighthouse eyes
Spirit flies.

Time warp matter
Spiraling laughter
Dancing time
Talking mime.

Planet tickle
Heart's fickle
Turn the page
Fall off the stage.

Flip the switch
Miss a stitch
Plan a day
Pass away.

Flute

The flute speaks
Listen to the wind
It plays
It flies with birds
It is a butterfly.
It is a bee landing
On a flower.
Sweet breeze
Blows through the flute.

Healing your spirit
With songs.

Yellow Flowers & Malbec Wine

Baked Cajun sole
Embraced by curried rice
Shared with a friend
At an unrushed lunch.

I listen to her animated story
While a sciatic nerve
Surges down my left leg
Throbbing in a spasmodic calf.
Yellow flowers and Malbec wine
Complement a soulful exchange.

Before she arrived, sleep whispered.
Last night I fell asleep
To the local news.

I woke up at midnight
To Jay Leno.
Too late for Howard Stern.

Next time I'll invite her
Over for dinner
And some telepathic play.

Years Past

Turning on the windshield wipers.
The years are speeding
Exceeding the limit.
The past rains on
The windshield
Every drop a memory.

I no longer see the road,
The moment.
I no longer believe
I can change my fate
Completely in one lifetime.

I am willing to accept
The road ahead as Is.
Yet I daydream about
What I'd like to be doing,
My ideal life, destination ahead-now.
I re-center in awareness.

Through the Light-Dark

Magic mystery time
Events glimpse heartbeats
Through the light-dark.
Time frame joy
Purpose destiny happens,

Moving on to the heart
Of the matter.

Today Is a Good Day to Die

Today is a good day to die,
Feeling the rush of the last sigh.
Gently launched to the far shore,
The light brightens more and more.

Today is a good day to die,
Time's up, saying goodbye.
Riding the timeless wave,
Emerging from Earth's cave.

Today is a good day to die,
Here's why,
Dying brings life to a close
Living balances with repose.

Today is a good day to die,
Listen – that's go lie.
My body is dropping away.
I'm grateful for its long stay.

Today is a good day to die,
The silver cord unties.
Lessons learned, wisdom gains.
Life ends, no more pains.

Upside Down & Backwards

The wacky, the weird,
The wonderful,
Upside down backwards,
Reverse forward,
The front of the back
The north side of the South Pole
Top of bottom,
The bottom of top,
Left side of right,
The right side of left,
Smell the taste,
See the hear,
Touch with the eyes,
Taste the color,
That's the inside out of it.

The Quiver

I park my old model car,
A midnight black ford,
She's my mechanical woman.
And I step out
Onto a vastless plain
Kansas, service station of America and shout,
"Your plains are dry,
An empty tumble weed bed."

I must be a neon light
To have the power of electricity,
My grave has electric coils,
Oh, what a pity!
I pop up
Like a piece of toast,
A heated ghost,
In the shape of an English muffin,
A miniature moon
The spacemen eat for noon.

My car is an empty grave,
My woman doesn't behave.

Topeka, Kansas is growing
As bright as a metropolis can.

I am an empty pop bottle,
Waiting to be picked up,
Washed and refilled.
Many of my pop bottle friends
Have been killed.
Broken glass everywhere
But they don't care.
Now they're pop top cans.

I can imagine staring up and up
To see tiny spaceships
Cutting through the emptiness of space
Like a laser into the eye of a blindman.
My lip quivers, I dare say,
"What do I need with gravity."

The Teaching Profession

Roses are red,
Violets are blue
In the teaching profession
There's lots to do.
The students will watch,
Actions speak louder than words.
The way you model
Creates dropouts or nerds.
It won't be easy,
You'll have to grapple.
Stick with the plan
And you'll receive your apple.
Bluffing is the heart
Of the game of poker.
If you bluff as a teacher,
You'll become a joker.
Teachers must deal
With the sorting machine.
Remember, students are not numbers;
They're living human beings.
When push comes to shove,
Teaching will require
Putting on your kid gloves.
Using fear in school,
Too much, and you're a fool.
Thinking things through
Is the teacher's way.
Beyond black and white

And into the gray.
Roses are red,
Violets are blue.
In the teaching profession
There's lots to do.

So. Cal Boy

My son is 19
LA image boy
BMW nightmare
Ship ahoy.
Living So Cal Boy
Sick Reno Wooster,
"I want a BMW dream."
Freshman, Malibu, Pepperdine
Fraternity, paternity
Maternity, patricide
Matricide, Sigma Nu.
Secret knock and handshake
Condom conscious yoga
For the 21st century.
My son is 19
A cheerleader mind
Gripped by teasing breasts
And west coast cum,
Blow job dreams.

Spinning Blue Ink

Spinning blue ink on white paper,
Random thoughts
Invoke the archangels
While drinking distilled water.

Bloodshot eyes after a steam,
A graduation party,
A crowd of one
Screaming a whisper.

Writing,
A serpentine motion
Through my intestinal mind.
I love carbs more than protein.

Four cheese pizza
After running a 7-minute mile.
A Hollywood player
Whimpering an alchemical mix
Of Vicodin, pot, and cabernet.

Snowflakes Melting on a Fiery Altar

A Sunday cheese omelet
And five cups of black coffee.
Warm sun, red leaves.

Strolling through a campus labyrinth.
I'm home inside myself.
Here among the brick, mortar, and brains.
Words drift like windless snowflakes
Through my head and feet.

I touch the present with empathy.
No past regrets,
No fear of the future.
I'm home inside myself
Sitting by the fire
Sipping creative ideas
And energized images.

Rare cathedral moments
Transform my spine into a spire
While windless snowflakes fall
Melting on a fiery altar.

Running a Red Light

I cleaned out my closet
Found a double helix
Blue ancient box
Opening it I escape
Through invisible walls
Into a forest
Of 100-year-old trees.
I shook a tree
Waking a female squirrel
Mt. Shasta erupted

Setting off an avalanche of trees
Ash rain burned my arms and legs
I launched a boat on Lake Minnetonka.
She appeared asking,
"How old are you?"
Forty-five, I replied.
You look 26
I like that you're wearing plaid.

Cool Ocean Beach

Cool Ocean Beach,
Toward the future reach.
No work, no play,
Only peace inside
Each day.

Root Canal for Dummies

I'm hippied out.
Tired of the Bingo-phobics
And the techtarded.
I surfed fat-pie.com.
Watched a blue
Seven-person bike
Pass by on Forest Street.
Been to the digital universe.
It will take care of you,
And here's the tricky part,

If you just let it.
Reminds me of what my mama
Used to say, "Nothing doesn't cost anything."
Stop and smell the Crayolas
And drink Cuban Mojitos
On the playa.
Experienced death by Hollywood
While reading *Root Canal for Dummies.*
My ego got pissed off at me
For buying gas station coffee
At 3 in the afternoon.
Learning that life is too short
To be sorry.
Proposing to never
Ask you to marry me.
Don't you find that muralesque?

Screw in the Lightbulb

I want to invest
All my time-energy
In the transformation
Of the daily bump and grind
The life of crime
Into the rhythm and rhyme
Of eternal time
Of Light, Love and Wisdom.

I want to be enlightened,
A beacon lighting the way

Out of the unlighted night,
No moon, no stars, no electricity.

I want to screw in the lightbulb
And turn on the power
Minute by minute, hour by hour.
Standing forever in a shower
Of light, love, and compassion.
Experiencing the grace
Changing my face
Holding an ace
Of hearts.

Pink i-Pod

Music kisses ear drums,
The beat raises waxed eyebrows.
Red painted toes tingle.
The lyrics, clear as mountain air,
Illumine a cave mind in pink.
Her electronic digital curves
Expand and contract, breathing.
The mall her temple,
A pink i-pod her soul,
Shopping her holy communion.
Images form in the pink glow,
Fashion illusions, the un-golden mean,
Disproportionate beauty,
Like dry vomit on fresh cement.
Cut and ragged jeans, 250 dollars,
Designer t-shirts, 80 dollars.

The kisses intensify,
The lyrics drown in a decibel sea.
A pink American Express card,
Her ticket to a perfect
Digital heaven.
Out of the Random

She had braces twice.
After a shot of bubblegum vodka
She blew herself to Venus.
It was so quiet she could hear a deck
Of cards being shuffled next door.
Then she really got Buddhist on me.
I offered her a bitch pop.
She wanted another shot
Of bubblegum vodka.
All the air came out of my ego.
"I really don't want to know
Anything about you.
I want to start with a clean slate.
Excuse me, your life is waiting
And I hear you can talk your way
Out of a sunburn.
Tell me, how can we
Plot our future together,
Or it was nice not meeting you."
"I'll have an ice water, please
With an ice garnish – ice ilicious!"
I'm not looking for a girlfriend.
I'm looking for someone who's not a flake."
We tried hard to be atheists.

Not I

Thinking thoughts others think.
Feeling feelings others feel.
Speaking words others say.
Doing what others do.
Evolutionary fields,
Cultural progressions.
Waves of thought, feeling
Words and actions.
The soul resonates experience;
Learning, changing.
Do *you* think thoughts?
Do *you* feel feelings?
Do you really say anything?
Do you really do anything?
Sometimes when someone talks
I don't hear anything.
They are not saying anything.
I hear sounds,
Empty words
They believe they say something.
Thinking, feeling, doing –
Why attach and "I" to it?

Money Tool

Money is a useful tool
Use it wisely or the fool.

It transforms need
To seed, to feed.

Money invested increases
Money spent decreases
Choose to be wealthy
Poverty is unhealthy.

There's more than enough for all,
Feeling lack you'll take a fall
Save for a rainy day,
Enjoy a Happy Birthday.
Making Ends Meet
Making ends meet,
Day and night.
Not ever quite making
Them meet.

So much time on
Bodily needs
Food to eat

A place to sleep,
A car to drive.

As you attempt
To make the ends
Meet, Be aware.
Just notice. Be conscious.

Then, even though the ends
Don't meet, you are present,
The Presence.

Lying About My Age

After running a red light
Cleaned out my bedroom closet
Found a forgotten
Ancient blue box
With an engraved double helix.

Gingerly cracked it open
Like a jack-in-the-box.
Wolves escaping through
Thick invisible walls
Into a forest of titanic
One-hundred-year-old sequoias.
With bare hands shook the top
Waking a female squirrel from her nest.

Mt. Shasta blew its whitecap
Firing an avalanche of trees,
Uprooting the earth.
Ash rain burned arms and legs.

Launched a rowboat
On the gold waters
Of Lake Minnetonka.

A young woman in a red velvet coat appeared.
"I like that you're wearing plaid," she complemented.
"How old are you?" she inquired.
"Forty-five," I answered.
"You look twenty-six."

Let's Dance

Feelings explode in gentle ripples
Warmed in the heart's grail.
There is no one else for me.
You have always been there – here.
Your presence is life
Flowing into and through my life.
Gentle, soft explosions of feeling
Shared in quiet moments
Between meaningful
Burst of speech.
We sip from the Holy Grail
Of our hearts
And taste the manna from heaven,
The sweet nectar of the gods.
Feeling all the love there is
Unleased through our souls.
Warm thoughts dance
Around one heart.
Your presence, whether here or there,
Is always now, no time, no distance.
The feelings are true
In a world where false
Is believed true.

Hold my hand sweet soul,
Share your true love
As I touch your heart
With a thought, a glance
A simple kind deed.
What we feel is rare,
Almost extinct.
Let's honor it
And show the world.
Let others feel our love
As we share our love.
One heart, one mind
Yet individual
Each nurturing each other's purpose.
Our time together is a treasure.
Sipping from the Holy Grail

Instagram Poems

Planetary beat
Heart rate races
Move your feet
Run the bases

The silence dance
Echoless sounds
High frequency trance
Consciousness abounds.

Turn, churn, burn
Conscious destiny create

Time boils to learn
Evaporates through heaven's gate

Speeding nonstop
A text travels first class

Star science embraced
Feel time erased
Go with lighted wings
Tibetan bell rings

Silent stones soften in the sun
Frozen fire burns as loud as hell.

Earth flights
Road trips
Set your sights
Get a grip.

Pool ocean beach
Toward the future reach.
No work, no play
Only peace inside each day.

Light night
Dark sunrise
Rainbow sight
Timeless wise.

Quiet Beach
Mountain stream

Feel the peace
On the light beam

Love and Light
Radiate from your heart.
Your aura bright
A mind so smart.
A manifest higher being
A goddess thru and thru.
A spiritual queen
Your thoughts and words are true.

In deep dirt
I become a life seed
Water, Light & Air
Alive, I am freed.

In between breathes
Feel the golden light
Regenerate a trillion cells,
Diamond stars at night.

Play in the now time
Moment to moment mime
Words and images poof
Feelings that need no proof.

Feel the silent surge
Of organic light
Charge body cells
With star might.

Liquid Time
Earthly Space

Launch, Climb
Gravity Outpace.

Dream clear
Releases fear.
Feel alive,
That's no jive.

2021, Happy New Year
Silence, listen, listen.
Joy, Love you hear
Body, mind, soul glisten.

Light beams
Thought dreams.
Magic places,
Happy faces.

Mystical image,
Time tells.
Whisper silence,
Tibetan bells.

Spiral flame,
Star's name.
Speed of light,
Thoughts write.

When you feel
Your heart
Energies heal,
Share the zeal.

The waves splash,
Moon beat.
Pisces rules the feet,
The fishes swim from the ashes.

Time expands
In your hands.
A billion light years
Ringing in your ears.

I'm passionate
About living
Because every day
There's giving,
Writing, and teaching
Into the future time
Makes me happy
That's my rhyme.

Felt the pain
Pleasure too.
Love is both
At the same time.
Yin is yang,
Yang is yin
Feel alive

Arrive
In the NOW.

Old Age Ain't No Place for Sissies

The 1930s and 40s movie star,
Betty Davis is quoted as saying,
"Old Age Aint No Place for Sissies."

Until I had my first hip replacement
I didn't know what she meant.
I've had both replaced now.
I know what she means.

I never knew much about pharmacies.
And what the word Meds meant.
Now I take seven meds a day.
Some pills are so small
They are hard to pick up.
When they fall on the floor
My cat eats them.
He doesn't have arthritis anymore.

Old Age Ain't No Place for Sissies.

I like to walk along the Truckee River
By Idlewild Park.
One day after walking 15 minutes,
My left foot began to fall asleep.

The doctor's diagnosis,
I had Radiculopathy,

It's a pinched nerve.
I can't pronounce it.
It's ridiculous.

Old Age Ain't No Place for Sissies.

Never been to ER.
Been three times this year.
I'm a regular.
They call me by my first name.

Old Age Ain't No Place for Sissies.

Now, I have a doctor appointment
Most every week.
This week they found out
That my heart ejection ratio
Went from 20% to 66%

Spiritual Frequencies Online Academy – Where you can become a Patron for a modest monthly subscription. Hundreds of Posts. Go to Patreon.com/spiritualfrequencies

Patreon: patreon.com/spiritualfrequencies

Email: spiritualfrequenciesonline@gmail.com

Instagram: drgfrequencies

YouTube: Greg Nielsen@DrG

Venmo: contribute directly to Conscious Books & Spiritual Frequencies Online Academy @Greg-Nielsen-9

Conscious Books
316 California Avenue, Ste. 210
Reno, Nevada 89509
U.S.A.

For an astrological chart including birth charts and yearly forecasts and/or a mythological interpretation of a tattoo email
Dr. Greg Nielsen: greganielsen@gmail.com

www.ingramcontent.com/pod-product-compliance
Lightning Source LLC
Chambersburg PA
CBHW060437090426
42733CB00011B/2305